Great Works Instructional Guides for Literature

THE CAT IN THE HAT

A guide for the book by Dr. Seuss
Great Works Author: Tracy Pearce

SHELL EDUCATION

Publishing Credits

Owen Pearce, *Contributing Author*

Image Credits

Shutterstock (cover; pages 12, 20, 22, 29, 31, 38, 48, 69–70); Timothy J. Bradley (pages 19, 46, 55)

Standards

© 2007 Teachers of English to Speakers of Other Languages, Inc. (TESOL)
© 2007 Board of Regents of the University of Wisconsin System. World-Class Instructional Design and Assessment (WIDA)
© Copyright 2010. National Governors Association Center for Best Practices and Council of Chief State School Officers.
All rights reserved.

Shell Education

5301 Oceanus Drive
Huntington Beach, CA 92649-1030
http://www.shelleducation.com
ISBN 978-1-4258-8954-8
© 2015 Shell Educational Publishing, Inc.

Table of contents

How to Use This Literature Guide

Today's standards demand rigor and relevance in the reading of complex texts. The units in this series guide teachers in a rich and deep exploration of worthwhile works of literature for classroom study. The most rigorous instruction can also be interesting and engaging!

Many current strategies for effective literacy instruction have been incorporated into these instructional guides for literature. Throughout the units, text-dependent questions are used to determine comprehension of the book as well as student interpretation of the vocabulary words. The books chosen for the series are complex and are exemplars of carefully crafted works of literature. Close reading is used throughout the units to guide students toward revisiting the text and using textual evidence to respond to prompts orally and in writing. Students must analyze the story elements in multiple assignments for each section of the book. All of these strategies work together to rigorously guide students through their study of literature.

The next few pages describe how to use this guide for a purposeful and meaningful literature study. Each section of this guide is set up in the same way to make it easier for you to implement the instruction in your classroom.

Theme Thoughts

The great works of literature used throughout this series have important themes that have been relevant to people for many years. Many of the themes will be discussed during the various sections of this instructional guide. However, it would also benefit students to have independent time to think about the key themes of the book.

Before students begin reading, have them complete the *Pre-Reading Theme Thoughts* (page 13). This graphic organizer will allow students to think about the themes outside the context of the story. They'll have the opportunity to evaluate statements based on important themes and defend their opinions. Be sure to keep students' papers for comparison to the *Post-Reading Theme Thoughts* (page 59). This graphic organizer is similar to the pre-reading activity. However, this time, students will be answering the questions from the point of view of one of the characters in the book. They have to think about how the character would feel about each statement and defend their thoughts. To conclude the activity, have students compare what they thought about the themes before they read the book to what the characters discovered during the story.

How to Use This Literature Guide (cont.)

Vocabulary

Each teacher reference vocabulary overview page has definitions and sentences about how key vocabulary words are used in the section. These words should be introduced and discussed with students. Students will use these words in different activities throughout the book.

On some of the vocabulary student pages, students are asked to answer text-related questions about vocabulary words from the sections. The following question stems will help you create your own vocabulary questions if you'd like to extend the discussion.

- How does this word describe _____'s character?
- How does this word connect to the problem in this story?
- How does this word help you understand the setting?
- Tell me how this word connects to the main idea of this story.
- What visual pictures does this word bring to your mind?
- Why do you think the author used this word?

At times, you may find that more work with the words will help students understand their meanings and importance. These quick vocabulary activities are a good way to further study the words.

- Students can play vocabulary concentration. Make one set of cards that has the words on them and another set with the definitions. Then, have students lay them out on the table and play concentration. The goal of the game is to match vocabulary words with their definitions. For early readers or English language learners, the two sets of cards could be the words and pictures of the words.
- Students can create word journal entries about the words. Students choose words they think are important and then describe why they think each word is important within the book. Early readers or English language learners could instead draw pictures about the words in a journal.
- Students can create puppets and use them to act out the vocabulary words from the stories. Students may also enjoy telling their own character-driven stories using vocabulary words from the original stories.

How to Use This Literature Guide (cont.)

Analyzing the Literature

After you have read each section with students, hold a small-group or whole-class discussion. Provided on the teacher reference page for each section are leveled questions. The questions are written at two levels of complexity to allow you to decide which questions best meet the needs of your students. The Level 1 questions are typically less abstract than the Level 2 questions. These questions are focused on the various story elements, such as character, setting, and plot. Be sure to add further questions as your students discuss what they've read. For each question, a few key points are provided for your reference as you discuss the book with students.

Reader Response

In today's classrooms, there are often great readers who are below average writers. So much time and energy is spent in classrooms getting students to read on grade level that little time is left to focus on writing skills. To help teachers include more writing in their daily literacy instruction, each section of this guide has a literature-based reader response prompt. Each of the three genres of writing is used in the reader responses within this guide: narrative, informative/explanatory, and opinion. Before students write, you may want to allow them time to draw pictures related to the topic. Book-themed writing paper is provided on pages 69–70 if your students need more space to write.

Guided Close Reading

Within each section of this guide, it is suggested that you closely reread a portion of the text with your students. Page numbers are given, but since some versions of the books may have different page numbers, the sections to be reread are described by location as well. After rereading the section, there are a few text-dependent questions to be answered by students.

Working space has been provided to help students prepare for the group discussion. They should record their thoughts and ideas on the activity page and refer to it during your discussion. Rather than just taking notes, you may want to require students to write complete responses to the questions before discussing them with you.

Encourage students to read one question at a time and then go back to the text and discover the answer. Work with students to ensure that they use the text to determine their answers rather than making unsupported inferences. Suggested answers are provided in the answer key.

How to Use This Literature Guide (cont.)

Guided close Reading (cont.)

The generic open-ended stems below can be used to write your own text-dependent questions if you would like to give students more practice.

- What words in the story support . . . ?
- What text helps you understand . . . ?
- Use the book to tell why _____ happens.
- Based on the events in the story, . . . ?
- Show me the part in the text that supports . . . .
- Use the text to tell why . . . .

Making connections

The activities in this section help students make cross-curricular connections to mathematics, science, social studies, fine arts, or other curricular areas. These activities require higher-order thinking skills from students but also allow for creative thinking.

Language Learning

A special section has been set aside to connect the literature to language conventions. Through these activities, students will have opportunities to practice the conventions of standard English grammar, usage, capitalization, and punctuation.

Story Elements

It is important to spend time discussing what the common story elements are in literature. Understanding the characters, setting, plot, and theme can increase students' comprehension and appreciation of the story. If teachers begin discussing these elements in early childhood, students will more likely internalize the concepts and look for the elements in their independent reading. Another very important reason for focusing on the story elements is that students will be better writers if they think about how the stories they read are constructed.

In the story elements activities, students are asked to create work related to the characters, setting, or plot. Consider having students complete only one of these activities. If you give students a choice on this assignment, each student can decide to complete the activity that most appeals to him or her. Different intelligences are used so that the activities are diverse and interesting to all students.

How to Use This Literature Guide (cont.)

Culminating Activity

At the end of this instructional guide is a creative culminating activity that allows students the opportunity to share what they've learned from reading the book. This activity is open ended so that students can push themselves to create their own great works within your language arts classroom.

Comprehension Assessment

The questions in this section require students to think about the book they've read as well as the words that were used in the book. Some questions are tied to quotations from the book to engage students and require them to think about the text as they answer the questions.

Response to Literature

Finally, students are asked to respond to the literature by drawing pictures and writing about the characters and stories. A suggested rubric is provided for teacher reference.

Correlation to the Standards

Shell Education is committed to producing educational materials that are research and standards based. As part of this effort, we have correlated all of our products to the academic standards of all 50 states, the District of Columbia, the Department of Defense Dependents Schools, and all Canadian provinces.

Purpose and Intent of Standards

Standards are designed to focus instruction and guide adoption of curricula. Standards are statements that describe the criteria necessary for students to meet specific academic goals. They define the knowledge, skills, and content students should acquire at each level. Standards are also used to develop standardized tests to evaluate students' academic progress. Teachers are required to demonstrate how their lessons meet standards. Standards are used in the development of all of our products, so educators can be assured they meet high academic standards.

How to Find Standards Correlations

To print a customized correlation report of this product for your state, visit our website at http://www.shelleducation.com and follow the online directions. If you require assistance in printing correlation reports, please contact our Customer Service Department at 1-877-777-3450.

correlation to the Standards (cont.)

Standards correlation chart

The lessons in this book were written to support the Common Core College and Career Readiness Anchor Standards. The following chart indicates which lessons address the anchor standards.

Common Core College and Career Readiness Anchor Standard	Section
CCSS.ELA-Literacy.CCRA.R.1—Read closely to determine what the text says explicitly and to make logical inferences from it; cite specific textual evidence when writing or speaking to support conclusions drawn from the text.	Guided Close Reading Sections 1–5; Story Elements Sections 1–5; Culminating Activity
CCSS.ELA-Literacy.CCRA.R.2—Determine central ideas or themes of a text and analyze their development; summarize the key supporting details and ideas.	Analyzing the Literature Sections 1–5; Guided Close Reading Sections 1–5; Post-Reading Response to Literature; Culminating Activity
CCSS.ELA-Literacy.CCRA.R.3—Analyze how and why individuals, events, or ideas develop and interact over the course of a text.	Analyzing the Literature Sections 1–5; Guided Close Reading Sections 1–5; Story Elements Sections 2–5; Post-Reading Response to Literature
CCSS.ELA-Literacy.CCRA.R.4—Interpret words and phrases as they are used in a text, including determining technical, connotative, and figurative meanings, and analyze how specific word choices shape meaning or tone.	Vocabulary Sections 1–5; Guided Close Reading Sections 1–5; Language Learning Sections 2–3, 5
CCSS.ELA-Literacy.CCRA.W.1—Write arguments to support claims in an analysis of substantive topics or texts using valid reasoning and relevant and sufficient evidence.	Reader Response Sections 3, 5
CCSS.ELA-Literacy.CCRA.W.2—Write informative/explanatory texts to examine and convey complex ideas and information clearly and accurately through the effective selection, organization, and analysis of content.	Reader Response Section 4
CCSS.ELA-Literacy.CCRA.W.3—Write narratives to develop real or imagined experiences or events using effective technique, well-chosen details and well-structured event sequences.	Reader Response Sections 1–2; Story Elements Sections 4–5

correlation to the standards (cont.)

standards correlation chart (cont.)

Common Core College and Career Readiness Anchor Standard	Section
CCSS.ELA-Literacy.CCRA.W.4—Produce clear and coherent writing in which the development, organization, and style are appropriate to task, purpose, and audience.	Reader Response Sections 1–5; Making Connections Section 3; Language Learning Sections 1, 5; Story Elements Sections 1, 4–5; Culminating Activity
CCSS.ELA-Literacy.CCRA.L.1—Demonstrate command of the conventions of standard English grammar and usage when writing or speaking.	Guided Close Reading Sections 1–5; Reader Response Sections 1–5; Language Learning Sections 1, 4–5; Story Elements Section 5
CCSS.ELA-Literacy.CCRA.L.2—Demonstrate command of the conventions of standard English capitalization, punctuation, and spelling when writing.	Language Learning Sections 2, 4–5
CCSS.ELA-Literacy.CCRA.L.4—Determine or clarify the meaning of unknown and multiple-meaning words and phrases by using context clues, analyzing meaningful word parts, and consulting general and specialized reference materials, as appropriate.	Vocabulary Sections 1–5; Language Learning Section 2
CCSS.ELA-Literacy.CCRA.L.6—Acquire and use accurately a range of general academic and domain-specific words and phrases sufficient for reading, writing, speaking, and listening at the college and career readiness level; demonstrate independence in gathering vocabulary knowledge when encountering an unknown term important to comprehension or expression.	Vocabulary Sections 1–5; Culminating Activity

TESOL and WIDA standards

The lessons in this book promote English language development for English language learners. The following TESOL and WIDA English Language Development Standards are addressed through the activities in this book:

- **Standard 1:** English language learners communicate for social and instructional purposes within the school setting.

- **Standard 2:** English language learners communicate information, ideas and concepts necessary for academic success in the content area of language arts.

About the Author—Dr. Seuss

Theodor Seuss Geisel, more commonly known as Dr. Seuss, was born on March 2, 1904, in Springfield, Massachusetts. As a young boy, Geisel loved funny stories, drawing, and animals. He grew up near a zoo, which he would visit quite often. Geisel liked to draw the animals he saw there although his animals always looked a little different and strange. Geisel's parents encouraged their son's playful imagination but also taught him the importance of hard work and a good education.

In 1921, Geisel graduated from high school and left for Dartmouth College. There he drew cartoons for the college magazine called *Jack-o-Lantern*. Some of the cartoons were of imaginary animals while others showed people doing silly things.

Geisel graduated from college in 1925 and traveled to England to attend Oxford University where he studied literature. He was going to become a professor, yet Geisel's true passion was still drawing. His friend Helen Palmer told Geisel that he should be drawing for a living. Geisel took her advice and left Oxford. He returned to the United States to try and make his dreams come true. A short time later, Palmer and Geisel were married.

Many different magazines hired Geisel as a cartoonist. Then in 1937, his first book called *And to Think That I Saw It on Mulberry Street* was published under the name Dr. Seuss. Geisel wrote many more books for children over the years. In 1957, a publishing company asked Geisel to write a book for beginning readers. The publisher gave him a list of words to use. The book Geisel wrote became one of his most famous books of all time. It was called *The Cat in the Hat*.

Geisel continued to write children's books and even won the Pulitzer Prize in 1984. In 1990, he published his last book called *Oh, the Places You'll Go!* He passed away the following year. Geisel's famously funny and colorful stories continue to delight readers young and old. More than 600 million copies of his books have been sold worldwide.

More information about Dr. Seuss and his books can be found at the following websites:

- http://www.catinthehat.org
- http://www.seussville.com

Possible Texts for Text Comparisons

The Cat in the Hat Comes Back, *The Cat's Quizzer*, *I Can Read with My Eyes Shut*, and *Daisy-Head Mayzie* all have the Cat in the Hat as a character in the story and could be used for enriching text comparisons by the same author.

Book Summary of *The Cat in the Hat*

This book is the first in a series that features the Cat in the Hat. Two bored children are sitting looking out the window as it rains outside. A mischievous cat wearing a tall, red and white striped hat enters into the home of Sally and her older brother. The Cat in the Hat performs many wacky tricks to amuse the children. The children's fish keeps telling the children that the cat should not be there when their mother is not home. However, the Cat in the Hat does even more tricks. Then, the Cat in the Hat brings in a box from outside and things get even more out of control. Two creatures named Thing One and Thing Two come out of the box. They bring out a kite and even more chaos occurs. Just before the mother returns home, the Cat in the Hat miraculously cleans up the house and disappears.

Cross-Curricular Connection

This book can be used in a science unit on rain or in a language arts unit on rhyming.

Possible Texts for Text Sets

- Ashman, Linda. *Rain!* HMH Books for Young Readers, 2013.
- Branley, Frankly M. *Down Comes the Rain*. HarperCollins, 1997.
- Miles, Elizabeth. *Watching the Weather: Rain*. Heinemann First Library, 2004.
- Sherman, Josepha. *Splish! Splash!: A Book About Rain*. Nonfiction Picture Books, 2003.
- Yee, Wong Herbert. *Who Likes Rain?* Henry Holt and Co., 2007.

or

- Dewdney, Anna. *Llama Llama Red Pajama*. Viking, 2005.
- Donaldson, Julia. *The Rhyming Rabbit*. MacMillan Children's Books, 2011.
- Keeler, Patricia, and Francis McCall. *A Huge Hog Is a Big Pig: A Rhyming Word Game*. Greenwillow Books, 2002.

Pre-Reading Theme Thoughts

Directions: Read each statement. Draw a picture of a happy face or a sad face. The face should show how you feel about the statement. Then, use words to say why you feel this way.

Statement	How Do You Feel? ☺ ☹	Why Do You Feel This Way?
You should not let strangers into your home.		
It is boring when it rains.		
It is important to pick up all your toys.		
You have to stay inside when it rains.		

Vocabulary Overview

Key words and phrases from this section are provided below with definitions and sentences about how the words are used in the story. Introduce and discuss these important vocabulary words with students. If you think these words or other words in the story warrant more time devoted to them, there are suggestions in the introduction for other vocabulary activities (page 5).

Word	Definition	Sentence about Text
shine (p. 1)	to give off light	The sun does not **shine** at Sally's house.
wet (p. 1)	soaked with water	It is too **wet** for Sally and her brother to play outside.
bump (p. 5)	an act of something hitting against something else	The **bump** they hear makes them jump!
step in (p. 6)	to move in a specified direction by lifting your foot and putting it down in a different place	The kids see the Cat in the Hat **step in** the house.
mat (p. 6)	a small piece of material used to cover the floor or ground	The Cat in the Hat steps in on the **mat**.
tricks (p. 8)	clever actions that someone performs to entertain people	The Cat in the Hat knows some **tricks**.
mind (p. 8)	to object to or dislike something	The Cat in the Hat says their mother will not **mind** the tricks.
away (p. 11)	from one place to another	The fish thinks the Cat in the Hat should go **away**.
about (p. 11)	in or near a particular area or place	The fish thinks the Cat in the Hat should not be **about**.
no fear (p. 12)	used to say that there is no reason to be afraid or worried	The Cat in the Hat says the kids should have **no fear**.

Vocabulary Activity

Directions: Choose at least two words from the story. Draw a picture that shows what these words mean. Label your picture.

Words from the Story

shine	wet	bump	step in	mat
tricks	mind	away	about	no fear

Directions: Answer this question.

1. Why does the fish want the Cat in the Hat to go **away**?

_____

_____

_____

_____

Analyzing the Literature

Provided below are discussion questions you can use in small groups, with the whole class, or for written assignments. Each question is written at two levels so you can choose the right question for each group of students. For each question, a few key points are provided for your reference as you discuss the book with students.

Story Element	Level 1	Level 2	Key Discussion Points
Plot	Why are Sally and her brother sitting in the house?	Describe what Sally and her brother are doing at the beginning of the story.	Sally and her brother are sitting at the window looking outside. It is too wet and cold to go outside. They can only sit in front of the window and look outside. They are not very happy about their situation.
Plot	What is the problem in this story?	Describe the problem in this story and make suggestions of what the children can do.	The problem is that the Cat in the Hat has just barged into the children's home. The children do not know what to do. At the very end of the section, the cat begins to play a game with the fish. He is obviously not listening to the fish's concerned warnings.
Setting	Describe the setting shown in the illustrations.	What words describe the setting?	The setting is the home of Sally and her brother. It is raining and cold outside. The Cat in the Hat looks very fancy with his umbrella, red bow tie, and red and white striped hat. The fish is also important since he does a lot of the talking in this section.
Character	How does the fish feel about the Cat in the Hat?	Using the text and illustrations, describe how the fish feels about the Cat in the Hat.	The fish wants the Cat in the Hat to go away. He thinks the cat should not be there when their mother is out. The fish wants to be put down and does not want to play a game of "Up-Up-Up with a fish." The fish is scared and is not having fun.

Reader Response

Think

In *The Cat in the Hat,* the children are bored because it is raining. Think about a time you wanted to go outside to play and you couldn't.

Narrative Writing Prompt

Write about a time you were bored because it was raining. Tell about what you did. Include some details, such as how you felt and what you did to end your boredom.

_____
_____
_____
_____
_____
_____
_____
_____
_____
_____
_____
_____

Name _____

Guided close Reading

Closely reread where the fish is talking to the Cat in the Hat (pages 10–13).

Directions: Think about these questions. In the space below, write ideas or draw pictures as you think. Be ready to share your answers.

❶ Explain why the fish thinks the Cat in the Hat should not be in the house.

❷ What is the name of the game the Cat in the Hat wants to play?

❸ Use the text to explain why the fish is right with his warnings.

Making connections—Rainy Day Fun

Directions: Sally and her brother are bored because it is raining outside and they cannot go out to play. Draw pictures of things you like to do when it rains so you are not bored. Label your pictures.

On a rainy day, I like to . . .

Name _____

Language Learning— Exclamation Marks

Directions: This story has many exclamation marks. Exclamation marks show excitement. Copy some sentences from this part of the story that have exclamation marks.

_____

- -

_____

- -

_____

- -

_____

- -

_____

- -

_____

- -

_____

Story Elements—Characters

Directions: Think about what you know about the characters in the book. Write at least two words or phrases that describe each character next to his or her name in the chart.

Sally	
Brother	
Fish	
Cat in the Hat	

Name _____

Story Elements—Setting

Directions: Write a five senses poem about the rain.

Use the frame below to help you write the poem.

Rain looks like _____.

Rain sounds like _____.

Rain smells like _____.

Rain tastes like _____.

Rain feels like _____.

Vocabulary Overview

Key words and phrases from this section are provided below with definitions and sentences about how the words are used in the story. Introduce and discuss these important vocabulary words with students. If you think these words or other words in the story warrant more time devoted to them, there are suggestions in the introduction for other vocabulary activities (page 5).

Word	Definition	Sentence about Text
high (p. 14)	rising or extending upward a great distance	The cat holds the fish up **high**.
rake (p. 18)	a tool that has pieces at the end of a long handle and is used to gather leaves, break apart soil, make the ground smooth, etc.	The fish is on the **rake**.
fan (p. 18)	a flat device that is held in your hand and waved back and forth	The cat holds a red **fan** with his tail.
lit (p. 22)	to attack or criticize someone forcefully	The fish **lit** into the cat as he said he did not like it.
sank (p. 25)	used force to cause something to go into the ground or another surface	The cat **sinks** the children's toy ship.
deep (p. 25)	far into or below the surface of something	The Cat in the Hat sinks the toy ship **deep** in the cake.
shook up (p. 25)	shocked or frightened someone	The cat **shakes up** the house and the children.
bent (p. 25)	having a shape that is not straight	The cat **bends** the family's new rake.
fox (p. 28)	a fast, small, wild animal that is related to dogs and has a long pointed nose and a bushy tail	The Cat in the Hat ran as fast as a **fox**.
hook (p. 29)	a curved or bent tool for catching, holding, or pulling something	The red box is shut with a **hook**.

Name _____

Vocabulary Activity

Directions: Draw a picture for each vocabulary word.

rake	fan
hook	fox

Directions: Answer this question.

1. Which thing in the story is **bent**?

_____

- - - - - - - - - - - - - - - - - -

_____

Analyzing the Literature

Provided below are discussion questions you can use in small groups, with the whole class, or for written assignments. Each question is written at two levels so you can choose the right question for each group of students. For each question, a few key points are provided for your reference as you discuss the book with students.

Story Element	Level 1	Level 2	Key Discussion Points
Character	What happens to the fish in this section of the story?	Describe how the fish feels about the Cat in the Hat now.	The fish falls out of his fishbowl when the Cat in the Hat falls. The fish lands in a pot and says he does not like the cat's game. The fish is angry and is not having fun. He still thinks the cat should not be there when their mother is out.
Plot	What are some of the tricks that the Cat in the Hat does?	With help from the illustrations and the text, describe the tricks the Cat in the Hat does for the children.	The Cat in the Hat balances the fish on the umbrella, stands on a ball, holds a book in one hand, balances a cup and a cake on his hat, holds some milk on a dish with his foot, hops up and down on the ball, and holds a fan with his tail.
Setting	Describe the setting.	The setting of the story also includes things you can hear, smell, and touch. Use these sensory details to describe the setting.	The setting is very chaotic with many items being balanced on all the different body parts of the Cat in the Hat. There is water and milk sloshing out of different containers. There is lots of action with the cat hopping up and down on the ball and the fan on the tail. At the end of the section, the cat leaves the house and returns with a large red box. This will probably be an important part of the setting in the next section.
Plot	What does the Cat in the Hat get from outside?	Describe what the Cat in the Hat gets from outside and make a prediction of what will happen next.	The Cat in the Hat runs quickly outside. He comes back in with a big red wooden box. It is closed with a hook and has a new trick that he wants them to see. Student predictions will vary.

Name _____

Reader Response

Think

In *The Cat in the Hat,* the cat falls down. Think about a time when you fell down in public.

Narrative Writing Prompt

Write about a time when you fell down in front of other people. Tell about what happened. Include some details such as how you fell, if you were hurt, and who helped you.

_____

- -

_____

- -

_____

- -

_____

- -

_____

- -

_____

- -

_____

- -

_____

Guided close Reading

Closely reread where the cat falls and crashes to the ground (pages 20–23).

Directions: Think about these questions. In the space below, write ideas or draw pictures as you think. Be ready to share your answers.

❶ According to the book, what did the cat fall on?

❷ Look closely at the words and the pictures to describe how the fish comes down.

❸ What evidence from the book shows that the fish does not like the cat's tricks?

Name _____

Making connections— Cat in the Hat Math!

Directions: The Cat in the Hat does many tricks and holds up many items. See if you can help solve these math problems. Draw a picture of each problem and then solve it.

1. The Cat in the Hat holds a cup of milk, a cake, two books, a fish, an umbrella, and a toy ship. How many things is the Cat in the Hat holding?

2. The Cat in the Hat is holding up 10 things as he hops on the ball. He wants to hold 15 things all together. How many more things will he need to hold?

3. As he falls, the Cat in the Hat drops 12 things. Half of the things break. How many things break?

Language Learning—Similes

Directions: A simile compares two things using the words *like* or *as*. Similes help writers make their writing more interesting. In this story, the Cat in the Hat comes back in as fast as a fox. Read the beginning part of the similes below and finish them in your own words.

1. as quiet as a _____

2. as big as a _____

3. hot like a _____

4. as flat as a _____

5. small like a _____

Name _____

Story Elements—Plot

Directions: Cut apart the cards below. Glue them on another piece of paper in the order they happen in the story.

The cat comes down with a bump!	The fish falls into a pot!
The cat runs outside.	The cat holds the fish up high.
In the box are two Things.	The cat comes back with a big red box.

Story Elements—Setting

Directions: Pick your favorite scene. Draw or paint a picture of that setting. Include only details shown in the illustrations. Write two sentences describing your picture.

_____

- - - - - - - - - - - - - - - - - - -

_____

- - - - - - - - - - - - - - - - - - -

_____

- - - - - - - - - - - - - - - - - - -

_____

Vocabulary Overview

Key words and phrases from this section are provided below with definitions and sentences about how the words are used in the story. Introduce and discuss these important vocabulary words with students. If you think these words or other words in the story warrant more time devoted to them, there are suggestions in the introduction for other vocabulary activities (page 5).

Word	Definition	Sentence about Text
bite (p. 33)	to press down on or cut into someone or something with teeth	The Cat in the Hat says the Things will not **bite**.
pat (p. 37)	an act of lightly touching someone or something with your hand to show affection or approval	The cat gives the Things a **pat**.
tame (p. 37)	not wild; trained to obey people	The cat says the Things are **tame**.
kites (p. 38)	toys that are made of light frames covered with cloth, paper, or plastic; toys flown in the air at the end of a long string	The fish calls out that **kites** should not fly in the house!
hall (p. 40)	a long, narrow passage inside a building with doors that lead to rooms on the sides	Sally and her brother watch the Things run down the **hall**.
wall (p. 40)	the structure that forms the side of a room or building	The kites bump on the **wall**.
thump (p. 40)	to hit something and make a loud, deep sound	The kites make a **thump** on the wall.
gown (p. 42)	a dress that a woman wears to a special event	Mother's new **gown** is on the string of the kite.
dots (p. 42)	one of a series of spots that make a pattern, especially on fabric or clothing	The **dots** are pink, white, and red.
kicks (p. 45)	move your leg or legs in the air or in water especially in a strong or forceful way	The Things run around with jumps and **kicks**.

Vocabulary Activity

Directions: Complete each sentence below. Use one of the words listed.

Words from the Story

bite	pat	tame	kites	hall
wall	thump	gown	dots	kicks

1. Thing One and Thing Two will not _____ you.

2. They should not fly _____ in the house!

3. The kites bump on the _____ in the

   _____.

4. Mother's new _____ is on the kite string.

Directions: Answer this question.

5. What does the Cat in the Hat mean when he says that Thing One and Thing Two are **tame**?

_____

- -

_____

- -

_____

Analyzing the Literature

Provided below are discussion questions you can use in small groups, with the whole class, or for written assignments. Each question is written at two levels so you can choose the right question for each group of students. For each question, a few key points are provided for your reference as you discuss the book with students.

Story Element	Level 1	Level 2	Key Discussion Points
Setting	What is the setting of this section of the story?	Describe how the setting is different from other parts of the story.	The story takes place all through the house. The Things come out of the red wooden box and are running up and down the hall and through the bedrooms. Earlier, the story took place just in one of the front rooms of the house.
Character	Describe how the children feel about the Cat in the Hat, Thing One, and Thing Two.	The book does not say exactly how the children feel about the Things and the Cat in the Hat. Using the pictures, how do you think they feel?	Sally and her brother look concerned when the Things come out of the box. Almost every page of this part of the story shows the children with shocked looks on their faces. Sally and her brother look scared as they peer down the hallway with the kites hitting picture frames, tables, and vases.
Plot	What do Thing One and Thing Two do when they get out of the box?	Describe the tricks that Thing One and Thing Two do and where they go when they get out of the box.	Thing One and Thing Two run out of the box very fast, shake hands with the children, and fly kites in the house. They fly the kites down the hall and bump into tables, pictures, lights, beds, and Mother's gown.

Reader Response

Think

In *The Cat in the Hat*, Thing One and Thing Two fly kites in the house and knock things over. Think about whether or not that is a good idea.

Opinion Writing Prompt

Write about whether or not it is a good idea to fly kites in the house. Include reasons for your opinion.

_____

- -

_____

- -

_____

- -

_____

- -

_____

- -

_____

- -

_____

Name _____

Guided close Reading

Closely reread where Thing One and Thing Two exit the box and shake hands with the children (pages 32–35).

Directions: Think about these questions. In the space below, write ideas or draw pictures as you think. Be ready to share your answers.

❶ Based on the text, how do Sally and her brother feel about Thing One and Thing Two?

❷ What words in this scene support the idea that the fish still wants the characters to leave?

❸ Use the text to describe if Thing One and Thing Two are polite or rude.

Making connections—House Rules

Directions: Thing One and Thing Two run through the house with kites. The fish knows that they should not fly kites in the house. Write some of the rules that you must follow at your house.

_____

- _ _ _ _ _ _ _ _ _ _ _ _ _ _ _ _
_____
_____

- _ _ _ _ _ _ _ _ _ _ _ _ _ _ _ _
_____
_____

- _ _ _ _ _ _ _ _ _ _ _ _ _ _ _ _
_____
_____

- _ _ _ _ _ _ _ _ _ _ _ _ _ _ _ _
_____
_____

- _ _ _ _ _ _ _ _ _ _ _ _ _ _ _ _
_____
_____

- _ _ _ _ _ _ _ _ _ _ _ _ _ _ _ _
_____
_____

- _ _ _ _ _ _ _ _ _ _ _ _ _ _ _ _
_____
_____

- _ _ _ _ _ _ _ _ _ _ _ _ _ _ _ _
_____

Name _____

Language Learning—Rhyme Time

Directions: The Cat in the Hat likes to rhyme. Help him to rhyme by drawing pictures of things that rhyme with the pictures in the kites. Label your pictures.

hook

pot

cat

Story Elements—Plot

Directions: The events in a story are part of the plot. Match each sequence word with the correct event from this part of the story.

First

We see the two Things bump their kites on the wall.

Next

Thing One and Thing Two come out of the box.

Last

Sally and her brother shake hands with Thing One and Thing Two.

Name _____

Story Elements—Characters

Directions: Draw a picture of the fish in the pot. Write words around the fish that describe him. Think of descriptive words to tell about the fish.

Vocabulary Overview

Key words and phrases from this section are provided below with definitions and sentences about how the words are used in the story. Introduce and discuss these important vocabulary words with students. If you think these words or other words in the story warrant more time devoted to them, there are suggestions in the introduction for other vocabulary activities (page 5).

Word	Definition	Sentence about Text
shook (p. 47)	moved back and forth	The fish **shakes** with fear when he sees Mother.
near (p. 48)	close in distance to someone or something	The children's mother is very **near**.
rid (p. 48)	to no longer have or be bothered by someone or something that is unwanted	The fish cries out that they will have to get **rid** of Thing One and Thing Two.
net (p. 50)	a device that is used for catching or holding things	The narrator gets his **net** as fast as he can.
bet (p. 50)	to think that something will probably or certainly happen	He **bets** he can get Thing One and Thing Two with his net.
yet (p. 50)	at this time	The boy thinks he will get those Things **yet**!
shame (p. 53)	something that is regretted	The Cat in the Hat thinks it is a **shame** that the children don't like his game.
mess (p. 55)	something or someone that looks very dirty or untidy	The fish is worried that Mother will come and find the big **mess**.
playthings (p. 57)	toys	The Cat in the Hat always picks up his **playthings**.
strings (p. 58)	a long, thin piece of twisted thread that you use to attach things, tie things together, or hang things	The Cat in the Hat picks up many things, including the **strings**.

Name _____

Vocabulary Activity

Directions: Practice your writing skills. Write at least two sentences using words from the story. Make sure your sentences show what the words mean.

Words from the Story

shook	near	rid	net	bet
yet	shame	mess	playthings	strings

_____

_____

_____

_____

_____

_____

_____

_____

_____

Directions: Answer this question.

1. Describe how the **mess** is picked up.

_____

_____

_____

_____

Analyzing the Literature

Provided below are discussion questions you can use in small groups, with the whole class, or for written assignments. Each question is written at two levels so you can choose the right question for each group of students. For each question, a few key points are provided for your reference as you discuss the book with students.

Story Element	Level 1	Level 2	Key Discussion Points
Character	Who notices that Mother is near?	Describe how they notice that Mother is near and what is said.	The fish notices Mother is near when he looks out the window. The fish says, "Think of something to do! You will have to get rid of Thing One and Thing Two!"
Plot	How are Thing One and Thing Two caught?	Describe how Thing One and Thing Two are caught and how you think they feel when they are caught.	The boy quickly gets his net and lets it down with a plop. He catches them with his net and then tells the Cat in the Hat to pack up the Things and take them away. Based on the illustrations the Things look surprised.
Character	How does the Cat in the Hat feel when the Things are caught in the net?	Describe how the Cat in the Hat feels when the Things are caught in the net and what he says.	The Cat in the Hat looks very sad and he says, "You did not like our game . . . . What a shame!" It's all still a game to the cat.
Setting	What is the setting in this part of the story?	Describe how the setting changes throughout this part of the story.	The setting begins as a very chaotic mess from all the tricks that were done. It changes when the machine that the Cat in the Hat brings in picks up all the mess. The house is left in the same condition as the very beginning of the book.

Name _____

Reader Response

Think

In *The Cat in the Hat*, the cat cleans up after himself. Think about why you should clean up your toys, too.

Informative/Explanatory Writing Prompt

Write about why you have to clean up your toys when you are done playing with them. Explain why it is important to clean up and how you do it.

_____
- -
_____
_____
- -
_____
_____
- -
_____
_____
- -
_____
_____
- -
_____
_____

Guided close Reading

Closely reread where the fish realizes that Mother is almost home (pages 46–49).

Directions: Think about these questions. In the space below, write ideas or draw pictures as you think. Be ready to share your answers.

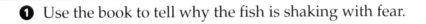

❶ Use the book to tell why the fish is shaking with fear.

❷ What questions does the fish ask after he sees Mother?

❸ Based on the book, what does the fish tell the children to do?

Name _____

Making connections—Pretty Patterns

Directions: There are patterns on the cat's hat and on Mother's new gown. Stripes and dots can be made into patterns that repeat. Make your own repeating patterns on the cat's hat and on Mother's gown.

Language Learning—
Alphabetical Order

Directions: Rewrite the list of the Cat in the Hat's playthings in alphabetical order. Draw a picture of each item in the box next to each word.

ship	books	gown
rake	milk	cake

1. _____

2. _____

3. _____

4. _____

5. _____

6. _____

Name _____

Story Elements—Plot

Directions: Write a new story. Pretend you live in the house, and the Cat in the Hat comes in with tricks to share. Write what you would say to the Cat in the Hat. Would you play tricks with him or send him away?

_____

_____

_____

_____

_____

_____

_____

_____

_____

_____

_____

_____

_____

_____

Name _____

Story Elements—characters

Directions: Write a song about how Thing One and Thing Two feel when they are caught under the net.

_____
- - - - - - - - - - - - - - - - - - - -
_____
_____
_____
- - - - - - - - - - - - - - - - - - - -
_____
_____
_____
- - - - - - - - - - - - - - - - - - - -
_____
_____
_____
- - - - - - - - - - - - - - - - - - - -
_____
_____
_____
- - - - - - - - - - - - - - - - - - - -
_____
_____
_____
- - - - - - - - - - - - - - - - - - - -
_____

Vocabulary Overview

Key words and phrases from this section are provided below with definitions and sentences about how the words are used in the story. Introduce and discuss these important vocabulary words with students. If you think these words or other words in the story warrant more time devoted to them, there are suggestions in the introduction for other vocabulary activities (page 5).

Word	Definition	Sentence about Text
sun (p. 1)	the star that Earth moves around and that gives Earth heat and light	The **sun** is not shining at the beginning of the story.
wish (p. 2)	to want something to be true or to happen	The narrator **wishes** he had something to do.
nothing (p. 2)	not anything; not a thing	The children feel like they have **nothing** to do.
down (p. 13)	from a higher to a lower place or position	The fish wants the Cat in the Hat to put him **down**.
ship (p. 16)	a large boat used for traveling long distances over the sea	The cat holds the toy **ship**.
dish (p. 16)	a shallow container that you cook or serve food in	The Cat in the Hat has some milk on a **dish**.
pot (p. 22)	a container that is used for storing or holding something	The fish fell into a **pot**.
bow (p. 31)	to bend at the waist	The Cat in the Hat **bows** to the children.
hit (p. 39)	to touch something in a forceful way	The kites **hit** the wall.
tip of his hat (p. 58)	to touch your hat or cap or to lift it off your head as a way of greeting or saying good-bye to someone	The Cat in the Hat is gone with a **tip of his hat**.

Vocabulary Activity

Directions: Draw lines to complete the sentences.

Beginnings of Sentences

We have **nothing**

Then he leaves

The **sun** is

The kites will

The fish falls

Endings of Sentences

into a **pot**.

hit the walls in the hall.

to do at all.

with a **tip of his hat**.

not shining.

Directions: Answer this question.

1. What does the cat do with the toy **ship**?

_____

- -

_____

- -

_____

Analyzing the Literature

Provided below are discussion questions you can use in small groups, with the whole class, or for written assignments. Each question is written at two levels so you can choose the right question for each group of students. For each question, a few key points are provided for your reference as you discuss the book with students.

Story Element	Level 1	Level 2	Key Discussion Points
Plot	What is the most exciting part of the story?	What is the problem in this story and how do the fish and the children try to solve it?	The problem is the Cat in the Hat is doing all sorts of tricks. He brings in Thing One and Thing Two, and they are running through the house, flying a kite, and bumping into everything. The fish keeps saying to get rid of the Things and the Cat in the Hat.
Character	What do you like best about the Cat in the Hat?	Describe the best parts of the Cat in the Hat's character.	The Cat in the Hat is exciting. He balances many things while he stands on a ball. He is very creative and tricky. He brings in Thing One and Thing Two for even more fun. He also quickly picks up the mess that he makes. He's magical.
Setting	Describe the setting throughout the story.	Describe how the setting changes throughout the entire book.	The setting begins with the children looking out the window of their house. It is raining outside. Very quickly, the setting changes into a very chaotic mess from all the tricks that are done. It changes again when the machine that the Cat in the Hat brings in picks up all the mess. The house is left in the same condition as the very beginning of the book.

Reader Response

Think

In *The Cat in the Hat* the mom asks, "Did you have any fun? Tell me. What did you do?" Think about what Sally and her brother should tell their mother about their day.

Opinion Writing Prompt

Write about whether Sally and her brother should tell their mother about the things that went on that day. Include reasons for your opinion.

_____

_____

_____

_____

_____

_____

_____

_____

_____

_____

_____

_____

_____

_____

Name _____

Guided close Reading

Closely reread where Thing One and Thing Two are caught in the net and are taken out of the house by the cat (pages 52–54).

Directions: Think about these questions. In the space below, write ideas or draw pictures as you think. Be ready to share your answers.

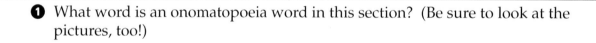

❶ What word is an onomatopoeia word in this section? (Be sure to look at the pictures, too!)

❷ Based on the text, what does the boy say to the cat?

❸ What words in the text show how the cat feels?

Name _____

Making connections—More or Less?

Directions: There are stripes on the cat's hat. Color a pattern of stripes on each hat below. Then, write a math problem using your pattern.

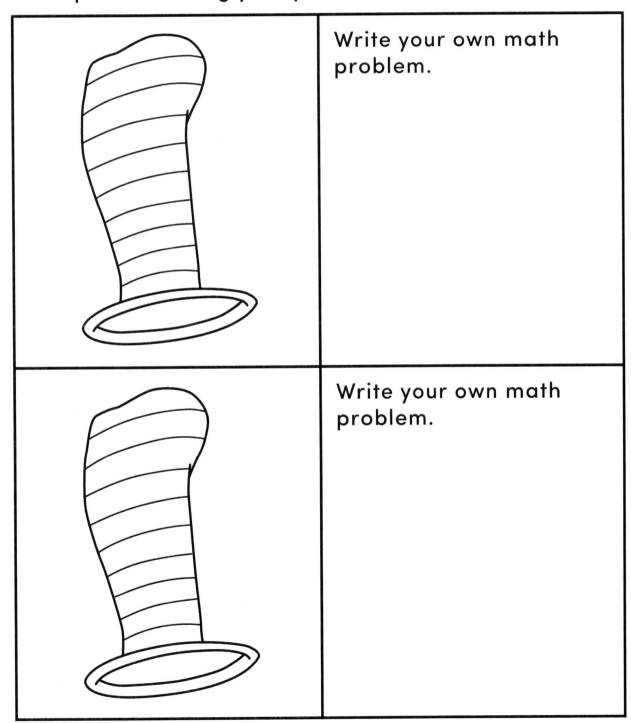

Write your own math problem.

Write your own math problem.

Name _____

Language Learning—
Rhyming couplets

Directions: Some books and many poems have words that rhyme with each other. *The Cat in the Hat* is a book that has many rhyming couplets. A rhyming couplet is two lines that rhyme. Write your own rhyming couplets to describe what happens in the story.

> Here is an example of a rhyming couplet:
>
> "Something went bump!
> How that bump made us jump!"

_____

- - - - - - - - - - - - - - - - - - - -

_____

- - - - - - - - - - - - - - - - - - - -

_____

- - - - - - - - - - - - - - - - - - - -

_____

- - - - - - - - - - - - - - - - - - - -

_____

Name _____

Story Elements—Plot

Directions: Stories have problems and solutions. Draw pictures to show the problem and the solution for this story. Label your pictures.

Problem   **Solution**

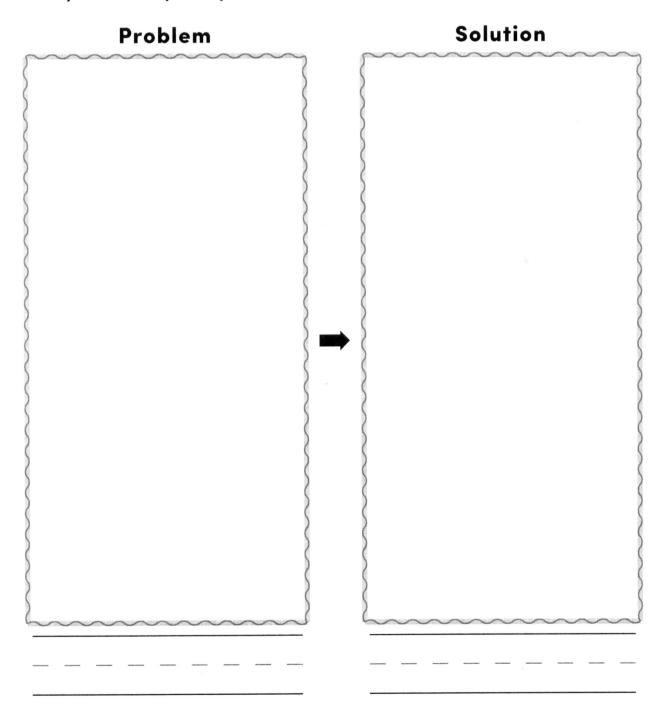

_____   _____

_ _ _ _ _ _ _ _ _ _ _ _ _ _   _ _ _ _ _ _ _ _ _ _ _ _ _ _

_____   _____

Name _____

Story Elements—Setting

Directions: Draw a picture of the setting at the beginning, middle, and end of the book.

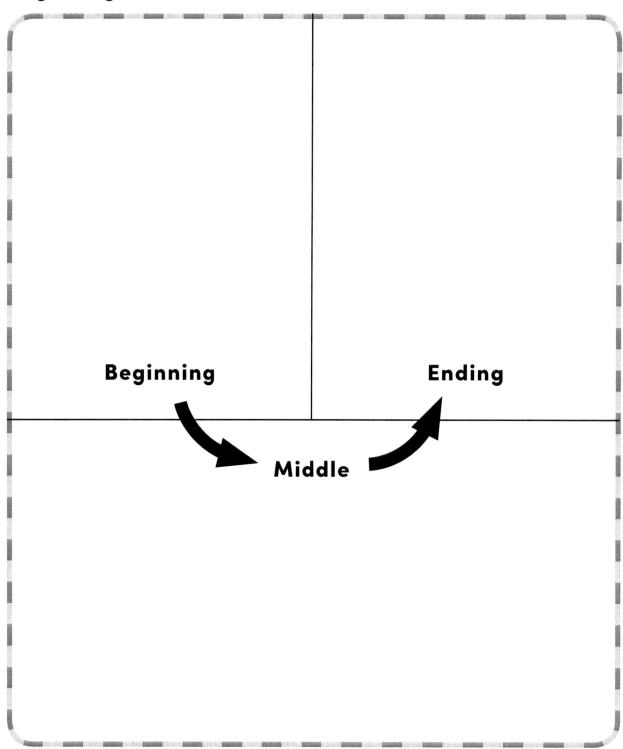

Post-Reading Theme Thoughts

Directions: Choose a main character from *The Cat in the Hat*. Pretend you are that character. Draw a picture of a happy face or a sad face to show how the character would feel about each statement. Then, use words to explain your picture.

Character I Chose _____

Statement	How Does the Character Feel? 😊 ☹️	Why Does the Character Feel This Way?
You should not let strangers into your home.		
It is boring when it rains.		
It is important to pick up all your toys.		
You have to stay inside when it rains.		

Culminating Activity: Fun with the Cat in the Hat

Directions: Work with students to help them choose one of the following activities. Most likely, these activities will require adult assistance to complete.

- Have students write and illustrate their own Cat in the Hat stories. Students can make their own stick puppets to use while they share their story.

- In small groups, students can practice and perform the reader's theater script on pages 61–63. Help students identify their parts on the script. Model for them how to read with expression. Have students think about how the characters would each talk. Let small groups of students take turns reading the parts and sharing the story with their peers.

- Let students experiment by retelling *The Cat in the Hat* in their own words. Students can make their own puppets to use while they retell the story.

- Have students decide which character is their favorite and create life-size figures. They should describe their characters and explain why they are their favorite characters from the story.

- In pairs, have students create three-dimensional models of the house from the story along with the characters. They may use supplies like construction paper, sticks, clay, craft sticks, or anything else they find helpful to display the setting and characters of the story. Then, they should use this model as a stage to recreate the story showing how the Cat in the Hat and the children interact throughout the story.

- Read some of Dr. Seuss's other books. Have students compare and contrast his other books to *The Cat in the Hat*.

Name _____

Too Hot to Play

Characters

Narrator   Brother   Sally
Cat in the Hat   Fish

Brother: The sun was shining.
                      It was too hot to play
                      Outside of our house
                      On this hot, sunny day!

Sally: Our mother made us stay in
                      And hide from the sun.
                      But inside of our house,
                      We never have fun.

Brother: Being stuck in the house
                      Is such a bore.

Narrator: The very next moment
                      There was a knock at the door.

Cat in the Hat: Hello, Hello, it's me,
                      The Cat in the Hat.
                      There is no doubt,
                      No doubt about that!

Fish: Oh, no! Oh, no!
                      This cat cannot stay.
                      Go back where you came from
                      On this hot, sunny day!

Too Hot to Play (cont.)

Cat in the Hat: I know this day is really hot.
So, I'll show you
How to make it not.

Brother: What trick have you brought
To cool us all down?
Hopefully they're not ones
That will make us all frown.

Fish: No, No!
This cat cannot stay!
Your mother is not here,
So please go away!

Cat in the Hat: This thing that I made
Is called a Thing-a-Ma-Bob.
With a flip of a switch
And a twist of a knob
It blows out cold stuff
As cold as freezing snow.

Sally: This snow is the ticket.
It is so much fun!
Let's turn the hallway
Into a winter sled run!

Fish: No! No!
This snow is a mess!
Watch out, Sally!
You'll get it on your dress!

Too Hot to Play (cont.)

Brother: Sorry, Cat!
But, you have to go.
Leave our house
And take all this snow!

Cat in the Hat: What a shame! What a shame!
I just wanted to play
And give you snow fun
On this hot sunny day.
It's time that I go.
I think I've overstayed.
But before I go,
I'll clean the mess I've made.

Narrator: With a flick of a switch
And a twist of a knob,
All the snow vanished
Into the Thing-a-Ma-Bob.

Sally: As the cat left,
Our mother arrived
With snow cones and ice cream.
What a cool surprise!

Narrator: Then Mother came in
And she said to these two,
"Did you have any fun?
Tell me. What did you do?"

Name _____

comprehension Assessment

Directions: Fill in the bubble for the best response to each question.

Section 1

1. What does the Cat in the Hat first say as he walks in the door?

   (A) "I know some new tricks."

   (B) "My tricks are not bad."

   (C) "Why we can have lots of good fun."

   (D) "Why do you sit there like that?"

Section 2

2. How does the Cat in the Hat react to the fish telling him to leave after the cat falls?

   (A) He says that he likes to be in the house.

   (B) He leaves the house.

   (C) He balances the fish on a rake again.

   (D) He puts the fish in a closet so he can't hear him.

Section 3

3. Why does the fish want the Things to leave?

   (A) He is sad that he isn't part of the fun.

   (B) He worries that they will make a mess.

   (C) He doesn't think they should be in the house without Mother.

   (D) He thinks they are strange.

comprehension Assessment *(cont.)*

Section 4

4. Why did the characters hurry to clean up the mess?

(A) The cat is sad that the games are over.

(B) Thing One and Thing Two have to go home.

(C) The boy catches the Things in a net.

(D) Mother is about to come home.

5. Describe how the mess is cleaned up.

_____

_____

_____

_____

_____

_____

_____

_____

_____

_____

_____

_____

_____

Name _____

Response to Literature: Sensory Details from *The Cat in the Hat*

Directions: Think about everything you can see, smell, hear, taste, and touch as you read *The Cat in the Hat*. Draw a picture of a scene from the story. Include all of the senses in your picture. Then, answer the questions on the next page about your scene. Make sure your picture is neat and is in color.

Name _____

Response to Literature: Sensory Details from *The Cat in the Hat* (cont.)

1. What is happening in the scene?

_____

- - - - - - - - - - - - - - - - - - - -

_____

_____

_____

_____

- - - - - - - - - - - - - - - - - - - -

_____

2. Why did you choose this scene?

_____

- - - - - - - - - - - - - - - - - - - -

_____

_____

- - - - - - - - - - - - - - - - - - - -

_____

3. What happens next in the story?

_____

- - - - - - - - - - - - - - - - - - - -

_____

_____

- - - - - - - - - - - - - - - - - - - -

_____

Name _____

Response to Literature Rubric

Directions: Use this rubric to evaluate student responses.

Great Job	Good Work	Keep Trying
☐ You answered all three questions completely. You included many details.	☐ You answered all three questions.	☐ You did not answer all three questions.
☐ Your handwriting is very neat. There are no spelling errors.	☐ Your handwriting can be neater. There are some spelling errors.	☐ Your handwriting is not very neat. There are many spelling errors.
☐ Your picture is neat and fully colored.	☐ Your picture is neat and some of it is colored.	☐ Your picture is not very neat and/or fully colored.
☐ Creativity is clear in both the picture and the writing.	☐ Creativity is clear in either the picture or the writing.	☐ There is not much creativity in either the picture or the writing.

Teacher Comments: _____

_____

_____

_____

Name _____

Name _____

The responses provided here are just examples of what students may answer. Many accurate responses are possible for the questions throughout this unit.

Vocabulary Activity—Section 1:
Pages 1–13 (page 15)
1. The fish wants the Cat in the Hat to go **away** because Mother is not there.

Guided Close Reading—Section 1:
Pages 1–13 (page 18)
1. "He should not be here when your mother is out!"
2. The game is called Up-Up-Up with a fish.
3. Students should discuss rules about strangers and why the kids should trust the fish's warnings.

Making Connections—Section 1:
Pages 1–13 (page 19)
Students' responses will vary, but responses should include pictures of things they like to do when it rains and each picture should be labeled.

Language Learning—Section 1:
Pages 1–13 (page 20)
Students' sentence choices from the story will vary, but responses should include sentences that use exclamations.

Story Elements—Section 1:
Pages 1–13 (page 21)
Students' responses will vary, but may include:
- Sally: bored, scared, jumped
- Brother: bored, scared, jumped
- Fish: fearful, scared, angry
- Cat in the Hat: tricky, funny

Vocabulary Activity—Section 2:
Pages 14–31 (page 24)
- Students' illustrations should match the vocabulary words.
1. The rake is **bent**.

Guided Close Reading—Section 2:
Pages 14–31 (page 27)
1. The cat falls on his head.
2. The fish falls into a pot.

3. The fish says, "This is not a good game. I do not like it! Not one little bit!"

Making Connections—Section 2:
Pages 14–31 (page 28)
1. 7 things
2. 5 more things
3. 6 things

Language Learning—Section 2:
Pages 14–31 (page 29)
Students' similes will vary, but should include comparisons that make sense.

Story Elements—Section 2:
Pages 14–31 (page 30)
- The cat holds the fish up high.
- The fish falls into the pot!
- The cat comes down with a bump!
- The cat runs outside.
- The cat comes back with a big red box.
- In the box are two Things.

Vocabulary Activity—Section 3:
Pages 32–45 (page 33)
1. Thing One and Thing Two will not **bite** you.
2. They should not fly **kites** in the house.
3. The kites bump on the **wall** in the **hall**.
4. Mother's new **gown** is on the kite string.
5. The Cat in the Hat says they are **tame** because they have come to play and have fun.

Guided Close Reading—Section 3:
Pages 32–45 (page 36)
1. Sally and her brother shake hands with Thing One and Thing Two, but they are not sure they want to.
2. The fish says, "They should not be here when your mother is out. Put them out!"
3. Thing One and Thing Two seem polite at first since they immediately want to shake hands with the children.

Language Learning—Section 3:
Pages 32–45 (page 38)

Students' illustrations will vary, but should include words that rhyme with hook, pot, and cat.

Story Elements—Section 3:
Pages 32–45 (page 39)

- **First:** Thing One and Thing Two come out of the box.
- **Next:** Sally and her brother shake hands with Thing One and Thing Two.
- **Last:** We see the two Things bump their kites on the wall.

Story Elements—Section 3:
Pages 32–45 (page 40)

Students' descriptions will vary, but the words they choose should clearly describe the fish.

Vocabulary Activity—Section 4:
Pages 46–61 (page 42)

The vocabulary words students choose will vary. Sentences will vary, as well.

1. The **mess** is picked up by the Cat in the Hat and a big red machine with many hands.

Guided Close Reading—Section 4:
Pages 46–61 (page 45)

1. The fish is shaking because he sees Mother is on her way home.
2. The fish asks the following questions: "Do you hear?" "Oh what will she do to us?" and "What will she say?"
3. The fish tells the children to do something fast and get rid of Thing One and Thing Two.

Language Learning—Section 4:
Pages 46–61 (page 47)

1. books
2. cake
3. gown
4. milk
5. rake
6. ship

Vocabulary Activity—Section 5:
Whole Book (page 51)

- We have **nothing** to do at all.
- Then he leaves with a **tip of his hat**.
- The **sun** is not shining.
- The kites will **hit** the walls in the hall.
- The fish falls into a **pot**.

1. The cat balances the toy **ship**, and then the **ship** sinks into the cake.

Guided Close Reading—Section 5:
Whole Book (page 54)

1. Plop!
2. The boy says, "Now you do as I say. You pack up those Things and you take them away!"
3. The cat says, "You do not like our game." "What a shame!" He also has a sad look.

Comprehension Assessment (pages 64–65)

1. D. "Why do you sit there like that?"
2. A. He says that he likes to be in the house.
3. C. He doesn't think they should be in the house without Mother.
4. D. Mother is about to come home.
5. The big mess is cleaned up by the Cat in the Hat and a big red machine with many hands.